Peace
Pilgrim's
Wisdom

Peace Pilgrim's Wisdom

A Very Simple Guide

Compiled by
Cheryl Canfield

BLUE DOVE PRESS | OCEAN TREE BOOKS
San Diego, California | Santa Fe, New Mexico

Books by Peace Pilgrim:
  Steps Toward Inner Peace
  Peace Pilgrim: Her Life and Work in Her Own Words

Materials about Peace Pilgrim are available in print and on tape in several languages. You can find out more about her life and message from Friends of Peace Pilgrim, 43480 Cedar Avenue, Hemet, CA 92544.

Copyright © 1996 by Cheryl Canfield
The actual writings of Peace Pilgrim included in this book are copyrighted only to prevent them being misused. People working for peace, spiritual development and the growth of human awareness have our willing permission to reproduce Peace Pilgrim's words.

FIRST EDITION. Printed in the United States of America.

Illustrations by Rena Paradis
Cover painting by Cliff Selover
  from a portrait photograph by Carla Annette
Design by Brian Moucka, Poppy Graphics

Published simultaneously in identical editions by:

OCEAN TREE BOOKS	BLUE DOVE PRESS
P.O. Box 1295	P.O. Box 261611
Santa Fe, N.M. 87504	San Diego, CA 92196
(505) 983-1412	(619) 271-0490
ISBN 0-943734-30-4	ISBN 1-884997-11-2

Library of Congress Cataloging in Publication data:

Peace pilgrim's wisdom: a very simple guide / compiled by Cheryl Canfield
        p.   cm.
   ISBN 0-943734-30-4 [1-884997-11-2]
   1. Peace of mind--Religious aspects--Meditations. 2. Peace--
Religious aspects--Meditations. 3. Meditations. 4. Devotional cal-
endars. 5. Peace Pilgrim, d. 1981--Quotations. I. Canfield, Cheryl,
1947-   .
BL65.P4P4324   1996
291.4'3--dc20   95-41443
                                                                        CIP

This book is dedicated to all seekers as an inspiration to look inside to the boundless wisdom of the still, small voice within – and to my parents, Archie and Alice Canfield, who knew and loved Peace Pilgrim, and have been guiding examples in an unconditionally loving partnership for fifty years.

*E*ACH SECTION OF THIS BOOK *opens with a "Travelogue," an excerpt from one of Peace's occasional Peace Pilgrim's Progress newsletters. In these she would share with friends her speaking plans, thoughts and insights on various subjects, and her observations and impressions of the states she had walked through.*

∞ Contents

∽ The Messenger

She strode out of the morning mist
As from the mist itself.
Such light shone bright from
   azure eyes
And silver threads enframed
   her face.

Stop! Where do you go
Old woman—
What brings you to
Our town?

Why, I've come to voice a message
That's been told throughout this age—
Time is short and come there must
An end to all this madness,
The killing and the hoarding
And the senselessness of slaughter.

And what have you
In your mannish garb,
All dressed in blue with
Lettered vest—
To say in way of guidance
That will lead us from our plight?

Why, not a thing that's new,
My friend,
I bear a message often told.
But humankind has waited long
To put these words to practice:

    Evil only duplicates
    When there is added more—
    Only good can overcome
    And lead away from war.

Such light shone bright from
Azure eyes,
Her words reverberated
So deep into our hearts and souls
That fear and hate abated.

*T*he messenger is Peace Pilgrim and, however one encounters her story, her pilgrimage reads more like the mythical tale of a traveling angel. I can attest that she was indeed a character of flesh and blood. I had the good fortune of knowing her quite intimately. Yet even as she walked this earth there were times when her presence created an impression of a spiritual stature that exceeded her physical form.

The first time I saw her she was striding through the large arch that framed the entrance to the Theosophical Society in Wheaton, Illinois. I watched her from a grove of trees some distance away and found myself startled by the way she seemed to fill the space that would ordinarily dwarf a large man.

It was in the spring of 1976 that I had this first glimpse of Peace. I had recently reordered the priorities in my life and the end result had brought me to this center where I hoped to get some insight into my own purpose. There must be something greater than the aim of "living the good life" that had been my focus before. In following that conventional path any sense of real fulfillment had eluded me and I found myself intrigued with idealistic thoughts that moved toward ways of collective responsibility.

I had read about the society with its national headquarters housing a staff of forty or so in a beautiful setting of trees and gardens. The motto of this group, "There is no religion higher than truth," was the beacon that drew me.

My desire at that time was to meet, in the flesh, an individual who was actually living the ideals I wanted so much to believe in, but I was still skeptical that the living of such ideals was humanly possible. The only characters of flawless virtue that I knew of were in books and I wanted tangible evidence that there was real chance of attainment in the process of growing toward the potential I was feeling inside.

When I watched Peace Pilgrim through the trees that day I felt a swelling sense of confirmation that my prayer had been answered. That evening she spoke to a small intimate group in the formal oak library. I watched her with a sense of wonder and admiration as she stood in the midst of our circle, her hands gesturing dramatically at every point as she told the story of her life. What stood out more than anything else was that here was an individual who was not just talking about the way things could be, but who was actually living the things she believed in. It was her life that gave so much power to her words.

If judged by appearance alone it would have been easy to dismiss her at first as some kind of kook. Her clothes were navy blue from her worn canvas sneakers up to the tailored shirt she wore beneath the faded blue tunic with large white letters that proclaimed her name on the front and her mission on the back. She spoke un-self consciously, completely absorbed in relating her story, her silver hair bouncing to the animation of her words.

She struck me as the most authentic individual I had ever met— yet despite that realness she was shrouded in a kind of mystery. The only name she gave was Peace Pilgrim and she wouldn't give her age, saying with conviction that she remained ageless by putting age out of her mind. It was easy for me to imagine that she had walked out of nowhere, an apparition of human potential. Her body was certainly aging despite her claim, but her agility and energy were remarkable. She had been criss-crossing the country on foot for over twenty years, counting more than 25,000 miles in the first ten years.

Her walking wasn't recreational, it was her occupation. She actually called it her "retirement project." She said her vow was to be "a wanderer, a pilgrim, until mankind learns the way of peace." In her vow she said she would walk on faith, and that was exactly what she had been doing all those years. She didn't carry money and she didn't accept money when it was offered. She kept her promise to "walk until given shelter and fast until given food."

Peace Pilgrim had started out with great determination and courage in 1953, during the McCarthy era, when war was raging in Korea and congressional committees considered people guilty until proven innocent. It was a time when there was a great deal of fear among people and it was safest to be apathetic. She considered it her calling to go forth in society, awake people from their apathy, and get them thinking. To draw attention away from herself and toward her message, she had renounced her personal identity and called herself only Peace Pilgrim.

In the beginning Peace emphasized that we "walk a knife-edge between complete chaos and a golden age, while strong forces push toward chaos. Unless we, the people of the world, awake from our lethargy and push firmly and quickly away from chaos, all that we cherish will be destroyed in the holocaust which will descend." At that time nuclear warheads were pointed at both the U.S. and the former U.S.S.R. and she felt that "all who are living today will help to make this choice, for the tide of world affairs now drifts in the direction of war and destruction." The message on the back of one of her earlier tunics read, "*WALKING COAST TO COAST FOR DISARMAMENT*" and later changed to "*25,000 MILES ON FOOT FOR PEACE.*"

She saw a truce in Korea that first year and continued walking through the unrest in the 1960s, the difficult days of Vietnam, and into the 1970s. Though she continued to speak about all aspects of the whole peace picture, her emphasis was that "ultimate peace begins within. When enough people find peace within there will be no more occasion for war."

When Peace began her pilgrimage she was an unknown. At the time I met her she had become such a popular speaker that her schedule was fixed two to three years in advance. She had no organizational backing but there were two or three individuals who forwarded her mail and sent out her little *Steps Toward Inner Peace* booklet to anyone who requested it. She said that the only time she took off was at Christmas, and she spent that time catching up on her correspondence and answering the extra mail she received during the holidays.

The message she spoke was simple but eloquent. Essentially, she talked about living the Golden Rule but she used her own words to describe it. "Overcome evil with good, falsehood with truth and hatred with love." There's nothing new in that, she would say, just in the *practice* of it.

I was struck by her radiance and countenance in those first few weeks as I accompanied her around the Chicago area where she had several speaking engagements on most days. I was with her when she spoke on radio shows, television talk programs, and at churches, universities, and public groups of all kinds. Her appeal was so broad that at an outdoor Catholic mass Peace's talk became the sermon. As I grew to know her over the years it continued to astonish me that so many diverse communities adopted her as their own.

There was no doubt that she was the reason I had come to the Theosophical Society. Only months before arriving I had given up my material possessions to pursue my prayer of finding a teacher and mentor for my spiritual quest. I had put my house up for sale and turned over the mortgage to the first couple who wanted it. Then I called the Salvation Army who had put out an appeal for household goods and asked them to send over a large truck to pick up the furniture in my four bedroom house. In the end, my husband, daughter and I packed our remaining belongings, mostly clothes, our young daughter's toys and the small dog we had kept as her companion, into our green Pontiac and headed east. The Pontiac, the only big possession we had kept, died in the salt flats just outside Salt Lake City. When we drove into the Theosophical Society it was in a rented van.

I left behind many things to be in Wheaton where my association and romance with Peace began. For the next five years my life became increasingly entwined with Peace Pilgrim. I accompanied her to Alaska in 1979 and to Hawaii in 1980 where she led the first of several planned inspirational and educational retreats. She told friends afterwards, "It's just a beautiful retreat situation. We're together for a couple of weeks amid beautiful surroundings and everybody comes back inspired and uplifted—everyone ready to work for their good cause." Just weeks before she died, Peace wrote to ask if I would accompany her the following summer when she planned to lead two retreats in the Pennsylvania area. I immediately wrote back that I would be honored to assist in any way. She never received my letter as "life's last glorious adventure" intervened.

Her mission started in 1953 and ended in 1981, twenty-eight and a half years later. She was so vital and strong that the end was a shock to those who knew her well. The circumstances at first seemed incongruous with her own sense of divine protection. The car in which she was riding to a speaking engagement was hit head on by another vehicle that had crossed the center line on a small two-lane highway.

I was stunned. Although Peace's message was simple there were so many levels of meaning and I felt there was still so much left to learn. In the days that followed I resolved to take time out alone to try to put together what I could about the impact of this extraordinary woman on my life. In time I discovered that she had left behind the most precious gift of all—the admonition to look within. "Your own inner teacher is within. You have all the answers inside yourself. Don't look to me. Look to your own inner teacher." Until she died I intellectually understood what she was saying but when I had questions I still went to her: "What can you tell me about this, Peace?" When she was no longer here I was forced to go within. To my surprise the answers came and continue coming. Just as she said, it's a resource that never dries up.

A few months after Peace died I received notice announcing a small memorial retreat in Santa Fe at the home of Richard Polese. Peace had left behind a mailing list of several friends who had connected with her over the years and Richard was offering an opportunity to get together to share our memories of special moments with Peace. This retreat took place over a period of ten days with people coming and going, exchanging stories, letters and other mementoes, and potluck meals. It was a beautiful and joyful time, much as Peace might have wanted it. Many people there wished that she had left behind a book so her words and life could continue to inspire and uplift a world so much in need of her simple wisdom and example.

At the end of the gathering five of us remained—Richard Polese, Ann and John Rush, Andrew Zupko, and myself. Together we recalled what Peace said just weeks before she died: "There has already been enough written. It just hasn't been put in book form." The inspiration was collectively embraced. Richard offered us the use of his house if we wanted to stay and put the book together and we unanimously agreed. Only months later, in 1982, the first edition of *Peace Pilgrim — Her Life and Work in Her Own Words* was completed. We published it ourselves. This original classic and Peace's own little booklet, *Steps Toward Inner Peace* are sent free to those who request it. My heartfelt

gratitude—and the gratitude of countless individuals who have bene-
fitted from reading the book—goes to Ann and John Rush, who have
devoted the entirety of their retirement years to the distribution of
Peace Pilgrim materials. John and Ann, with a handful of unpaid vol-
unteers and many donations, continue to make it possible. The book
and booklet are also available in Spanish and Russian. You can obtain
copies by writing to Friends of Peace Pilgrim, 43480 Cedar Avenue,
Hemet, California 92544, (909) 927-7678.

Whether *Peace Pilgrim's Wisdom* is your first introduction to
Peace or you are familiar with her life and work, you'll have a wonderful adventure in the pages ahead as you use these simple ideas as
seed thoughts for your own meditation.

Cheryl Canfield
Napa, California

How to Use this Book as a Study Guide

editations on the thoughts collected here provide a simple format and guide for study and self-reflection. The idea is not to accept them or to reject them, but to take them inside to reflect upon. There are 365 thoughts, one for each day of the year. You can start at any time right from the beginning or choose topics of special interest or current relevance to you.

Each day a thought can be used to ponder during a quiet moment. It is very centering to focus on the most meaningful and permanent aspects of life both in the morning, to set a tone for the day, and in the evening, to bring this focus into the restful hours of sleep.

For avid learners seeking to connect more strongly with the wonderful inner resources that are available when we find and listen to our own inner guidance, I suggest using this book in conjunction with or as a personal journal. Creating space for quiet reflection and journaling may well be the catalyst for making the best use of the rest of your life. Here is a simple system that can be most rewarding and powerful:

STEP ONE: Take a moment upon waking to read a thought for the day. Jot it down on a piece of paper or a note card and put it in a handy pocket or wallet that you can access during the day. Tell yourself to pull the thought out periodically during quiet moments and just read it. Your subconscious will automatically begin processing, developing and integrating the thought while your conscious mind attends to the details of your day's tasks.

STEP TWO: Set aside a time, even if only fifteen or twenty minutes, when you can be away from interruptions. Unplug the phone if necessary (or turn the ringer off and the answering machine on). Create a moment in which there is nothing more important than just being in a quiet, relaxed, receptive state.

STEP THREE: Read the thought for the day again, then take out your personal journal. Write whatever thoughts come to your mind in the beginning; you will be surprised how the thoughts keep developing and growing. As your journal entries grow with continuing practice you will have a record to look back on. With this retrospective view you will find your understanding and awareness growing and deepening at an accelerated pace.

You can use the space provided after each thought and at the end of this book to create your personal journal or you can take these seed thoughts inside for quiet reflection. Either way, you are embarking on an exciting inner journey. It has been a joy for me to put *Peace Pilgrim's Wisdom* together and my hope is that all those who read it will benefit from her simple wisdom.

If this book has a special impact on you or you want to share how it has connected with your life, you can write to Cheryl Canfield at P. O. Box 10231, Napa, California 94581.

Peace Pilgrim's Wisdom

Photograph by Jim Morrill, courtesy of Linda Ann Scott.

It is a joy to walk through California in the winter— through the warm sunshine of an irrigated desert, atop a cliff overlooking the blue Pacific or along a beach, through orchards and vineyards and nut groves and cultivated fields, over scenic mountain passes.

In Southern California trees seem sparse, although palm trees line the city streets and eucalyptus trees line the desert highways. Northern California, with its massive redwoods, seems to be a land of trees.

California is a land where seasons are not very pronounced and flowers often disregard the proper blooming time. It is not uncommon to see chrysanthemums, poinsettias and jonquils blooming happily with geraniums, petunias and other summer flowers.

∞ One...

The Spiritual Path

❀ 1 The universe is a school where people will eventually develop into the image and likeness of God. It will exist as long as a school is needed.

....

....

....

....

....

❀ 2 There is nothing that happens by chance in our universe. Everything unfolds according to higher laws—everything is regulated by divine order.

....

....

....

....

....

❦3 What we usually call human evolution is the awakening of the divine nature within us.

....
....
....
....
....

❦4 Your divine nature is there from the beginning of your evolution in human form. It is the real you—but in the beginning it is unawakened.

....
....
....
....
....

❦5 You cannot really know with your limited intelligence or with your five senses that there is more than the physical universe. But when you awaken the divine nature, it knows.

....
....
....
....
....

❦ 6 We can believe through having been taught—but we know through having perceived or having experienced.

....
....
....
....
....

❦ 7 Physical evolution takes place through adjustment to environment while spiritual evolution takes place through obedience to God's will.

....
....
....
....

❦ 8 The outer utopia would come when we have learned to share and not to kill each other. The inner utopia would come when we have all found inner peace. The first is foreseeable—the second will take a lot longer.

....
....
....
....
....

❦9 Spiritual evolution takes place in your life as you live in harmony with divine purpose—obeying divine laws, which are the same for all of us, and doing your own special job in the divine plan.

....
....
....
....

❦10 You have free will to choose between doing God's will and refusing to do God's will, but only God's will can bring harmony into your life.

....
....
....
....
....

❦11 The body, mind and emotions are instruments which can be used either by the self-centered nature or by the God-centered nature which is centered in the good of the whole.

....
....
....
....
....

❧ *12* Some spiritual truths can be intellectually understood—some cannot. The spiritual life is that which cannot be perceived by the five senses.

....

....

....

....

....

❧ *13* There is now a great interest in the inner search and as a result, there are many people who have made a start along the spiritual path.

....

....

....

....

....

❧ *14* The beginning of the spiritual growing up is the time when you feel completely willing, without any reservation, to give your life and to leave the self-centered life.

....

....

....

....

....

❧ 15 When you begin the spiritual growing up you go into direct struggle between the two natures—the God-centered nature and the self-centered nature—with the two different viewpoints.

....

....

....

....

❧ 16 There are hills and valleys in this time of spiritual growing up—and for some it is an ascending experience.

....

....

....

....

❧ 17 Every hilltop in the area of spiritual growth seems to get a little higher than the last hilltop, until you rise high enough in consciousness to look at the entire universe through the eyes of the God-centered nature.

....

....

....

....

❦18   The illumination experience is the first glimpse of what the life of inner peace is like. It is a feeling of complete and absolute oneness with all creation.

....
....
....
....

❦19   After the first glimpse of inner peace you slip in and out, and then you get onto the plateaus, where you are most of the time, and are only slipping out of harmony occasionally.

....
....
....
....

❦20   After a period of struggle, you reach the time when you succeed in changing your life; bringing your life into harmony or finding inner peace.

....
....
....
....
....

❦ 21 Inner peace or happiness will come to you when you have fulfilled the conditions of liberation.

....

....

....

....

....

❦ 22 There is no glimpse of the light without walking the path. You can't get it from anyone else, nor can you give it to anyone.

....

....

....

....

....

❦ 23 The spiritual growth pattern takes time, the same as any other growth pattern, and it was fifteen years before I had completed the spiritual growing up and found inner peace.

....

....

....

....

....

❧ **24** After finding inner peace you feel plugged in to the source of Universal supply which is what I live on.

....

....

....

....

....

❧ **25** When you find inner peace you feel plugged in to the source of universal truth which is endlessly available.

....

....

....

....

....

❧ **26** With inner peace you feel plugged in to the source of universal energy which is what I walk on.

....

....

....

....

....

....

❦27 You have that endless energy only insofar as you are working for the good of the whole. As soon as you start working for your little self it's gone. That's the secret of it. In this world you are given as you give.

....

....

....

....

❦28 Most human beings only scratch the surface of their real potential. They have no idea what they're capable of.

....

....

....

....

....

❦29 When you have come through the spiritual growing up, you discover that learning and growing do not cease. They continue harmoniously without struggle.

....

....

....

....

❧30 Once you have found inner peace it's as though the central figure of the jigsaw of your life is complete now and clear and unchanging. There is stability in your life but around the edges the pieces keep right on fitting in.

....
....
....
....

❧31 I remember the experience of the first glimpse of what the life of inner peace is like. I felt very uplifted, more uplifted than I had ever been, and I knew timelessness and spacelessness and lightness. I did not seem to be walking on the earth.

....
....
....
....

❧32 The most important part of my first experience of inner peace was the realization of the oneness of all creation—not only of all human beings.

....
....
....
....

❧33 In that first glimpse of inner peace I experienced oneness with the creatures that walk the earth, with the air, with the water, with the earth itself. And most wonderful of all—a oneness with that which many would call God.

....

....

....

....

❧34 When you have found inner peace the unimportant things seem very trivial; you wouldn't waste your time on them.

....

....

....

....

....

❧35 There are many hills and valleys on the spiritual path. The struggle is like climbing, with each hilltop a little higher than the last.

....

....

....

....

....

❦36 It is not an easy undertaking, but I can assure you that the end of your spiritual journey will be well worth the price paid.

....
....
....
....
....
....

❦37 Inner peace is something which is possible to find, whether in this earth life or beyond...

....
....
....
....
....
....

❦38 Nobody can prove that there is life after death. This is something that you can know only through an awakening of your divine nature.

....
....
....
....
....
....

❧39 If you understand that the soul not only has experience beyond the earth life but also had experience before the earth life, it is easier to understand why people are in varied stages of growth.

❧40 That which is received from without can be compared with knowledge. It leads to a believing, which is seldom strong enough to motivate to action. That which is confirmed from within can be compared with wisdom. It leads to a knowing, and action goes right along with it.

❧41 Truth is the pearl without price. One cannot obtain truth by buying it—all you can do is strive for spiritual truth and when one is ready, it will be given freely.

❦42 One who is in possession of spiritual truth would not be selling it, so one who is selling it doesn't have it.

....
....
....
....
....

❦43 You lose any spiritual contact if you commercialize on it. These are the "pearls without price."

....
....
....
....
....

❦44 Those who attempt to buy spiritual truth are trying to get it before they are ready. In this wonderfully well-ordered universe, when they are ready, it will be given.

....
....
....
....
....

❧45 I always think about the bud of a flower. If you give it proper conditions it will open into a beautiful flower, but if you are impatient and try to tear the petals open you permanently injure the flower.

....

....

....

....

❧46 The flower can be equated with the earthly human life. Give the spiritual growing-up the proper growing conditions and it will open into a thing of beauty.

....

....

....

....

....

❧47 When you feel the need of a spiritual lift, try getting to bed early and get up early to have a quiet time at dawn.

....

....

....

....

❦48 Overcome evil with good, falsehood with truth, and hatred with love. The message isn't new, but we haven't learned to live it yet.

....
....
....
....
....

❦49 Penance is the willingness to undergo hardships for the achievement of a good purpose.

....
....
....
....
....
....
....

❦50 It isn't more light we need, it's putting into practice what light we already have.

....
....
....
....
....
....

❦51 Great blessings lie in store for those who are wise enough to put into practice the highest light that comes to them.

....

....

....

....

....

❦52 Mature people live according to their highest light; they lead the way; they are the pioneers.

....

....

....

....

....

❦53 If you want to teach people, young or old, you must start where they are: at their level of understanding—and use words they understand. When you have captured their attention, you can take them as far as they are able to go.

....

....

....

....

....

❦54 If you perceive that others are already beyond your level of understanding, let them teach you.

....
....
....
....
....

❦55 Implanting spiritual ideas in children is very important. Many people live their entire lives according to the concepts that are implanted in them in childhood.

....
....
....
....
....

❦56 Parents should train their children through example—no other way will work.

....
....
....
....
....

❧57 Look within for your answers. Your divine nature—your inner light—knows all the answers.

....
....
....
....
....
....

❧58 Trust in your own inner voice. This is your guide, this is your teacher. Your teacher is within, not without. Know yourself.

....
....
....
....
....

❧59 The path of the seeker is full of pitfalls and temptations, and the seeker must walk it alone with God. Keep your feet on the ground and your thoughts at lofty heights.

....
....
....
....
....

❦ 60 Remember that the one who does an unworthy deed is in reality psychologically sick, and should be regarded with as much compassion as one who is physically sick.

....
....
....
....
....

❦ 61 All human beings are God's children and they could act that way. So I love them for what they could be or for what they really are.

....
....
....
....
....
....

When I began my walk in the West rhododendron was outstanding in the gardens and yellow broom was queen on the hillsides. I walked north along the fertile, rain-soaked west coasts of Oregon and Washington, surrounded by big beautiful trees. To the east were the Cascades, with Mount Hood towering on the Portland skyline and Mount Rainier towering on the Seattle skyline—on those happy occasions when they emerged from the clouds. To the west were the rugged Olympics.

I explored the scenic Columbia River Valley, and traveled up to meet a group of Canadian friends at Peace Arch Park between the two countries. West of the Cascades I have never seen more verdure. East of the Cascades there is sagebrush desert except where irrigation creates an oasis.

∞ Two...

Peace

❧ 62 Peace is much more than the temporary absence of war. It is the absence of the causes of war which are so much still with us in the world today.

❧ 63 The situation in the world around us is just a reflection of the collective situation. Only as we become more peaceful people will we be finding ourselves living in a more peaceful world.

❧64   Humanity, with fearful, faltering steps walks a knife-edge between abysmal chaos and a new renaissance, while strong forces push toward chaos. Yet there is hope.

....

....

....

....

....

❧65   I see hope in the tireless work of a few devoted souls; I see hope in the real desire for peace in the heart of humanity, even though the human family gropes toward peace blindly, not knowing the way.

....

....

....

....

❧66   Knowing that all things contrary to God's laws are transient, let us avoid despair and radiate hope for a warless world.

....

....

....

....

❦ 67 Let us never say hopelessly, "This is the darkness before a storm." Let us rather say with faith, "This is the darkness before the dawn of a Golden Age of peace which we cannot now even imagine." For *this* let us hope and work and pray.

....
....
....
....

❦ 68 My prayer is that this war-weary world of ours will somehow find the way to peace before a holocaust descends.

....
....
....
....
....

❦ 69 Peace and freedom—these things shall be. How soon these things shall be—whether now or whether after great destruction and new beginnings and aeons of time—is up to us.

....
....
....
....

❧ 70 All people can be peace workers. Whenever you bring harmony into any unpeaceful situation, you contribute to the total peace picture. Insofar as you have peace in your life, you reflect it into your world.

....
....
....
....

❧ 71 We people of the world need to learn to put the welfare of the whole human family above the welfare of any group.

....
....
....
....
....

❧ 72 A few really dedicated people can offset the ill effects of masses of out-of-harmony people, so we who work for peace must not falter.

....
....
....
....
....

73 We must continue to pray for peace and to act for peace in whatever way we can. We must continue to speak for peace and to live the way of peace.

....
....
....
....
....
....

74 To inspire others, we must continue to think of peace and to know it is possible. What we dwell upon we help to bring into manifestation.

....
....
....
....
....

75 What people really suffer from is immaturity. Among mature people war would not be a problem—it would be impossible.

....
....
....
....
....

76 If we were people who had done a full growing up, not only the mental and emotional but the spiritual growing up, we wouldn't have wars. We would have learned the lesson of sharing and the lesson of non-killing.

....
....
....
....

77 If I am killed, it destroys merely the clay garment, the body. But if I kill, it injures the reality, the soul.

....
....
....
....

78 This immaturity which the world suffers from manifests in things like greed, grabbing more than our share; in things like fear, which cause us to build up armaments against one another. These are the direct symptoms of our immaturity.

....
....
....
....

79 War is really a symptom of a symptom. It is a symptom of the fear which causes us to build up armaments which results in war.

....
....
....
....
....

80 Starvation is a symptom of a symptom. It is a symptom of the greed, which causes some to grab more than their share while others are starving.

....
....
....
....
....

81 In our immaturity we want, at the same time, peace and the things which make war.

....
....
....
....
....

❦ 82 The price of peace is obedience to the higher laws: evil can only be overcome by good and hatred by love; only a good means can attain a good end.

....
....
....
....
....

❦ 83 The price of peace is to abandon fear and replace it with faith—faith that if we obey God's laws we will receive God's blessings.

....
....
....
....
....

❦ 84 The price of peace is to abandon hate and allow love to reign supreme in our hearts—love for all our fellow human beings over the world.

....
....
....
....
....

85 The price of peace is to abandon greed and replace it with giving, so that none will be spiritually injured by having more than they need while others in the world have less than they need.

86 In a conflict situation you must be thinking of a solution which is fair to all concerned, instead of a solution which is of advantage to you. Only a solution which is fair to all concerned can be workable in the long run.

87 There is a magic formula for resolving conflicts. It is this: Have as your objective the resolving of the conflict—not the gaining of advantage.

❧88 There is a magic formula for avoiding conflicts. It is this: Be concerned that you do not offend, not that you are not offended.

....

....

....

....

❧89 The key word for our time is *practice*. We have all the light we need, we just need to put it into practice.

....

....

....

....

....

❧90 At this moment in history I feel that we are the most influential nation in the world and if we were to turn in the direction of peace and a better way of life, if we were to live our religious teachings, I think the world would follow.

....

....

....

....

....

❧91 Physical violence can end even before we have learned the way of love, but psychological violence will continue until we do. Only outer peace can be had through law. The way to inner peace is through love.

....

....

....

....

❧92 A world language would be the biggest single step we could take toward world understanding, and a long stride toward world peace. When we can talk together we will realize that our likenesses are much greater than our differences, however great our differences may seem.

....

....

....

....

....

....

....

In Montana I climbed the Rockies and crossed the Continental Divide. From Montana I went to visit Yellowstone Park for the first time and saw some amazing sights I had never seen before—geysers, steam vents, seething mud holes, boiling pools which were often very colorful—besides all the animals and the scenic beauty. In Idaho I walked along a river where great springs leaped from a canyon wall and cascaded into the stream. Whenever I enter Idaho I remember the remarkable display of spring wildflowers I enjoyed during my first walk there. In Utah—the Mormon State—I was given very fine hospitality—a bed every night and ample food. In Nevada I walked past steaming springs and past beautiful Lake Mead which is formed by Hoover Dam.

∞ Three...

God

93 There is a power greater than ourselves which manifests itself within us as well as everywhere else in the universe. This I call God.

....

....

....

....

....

94 God is the cause—everything else is an effect. You are an effect which has free will, but only over how soon you will be willing to live in harmony with divine purpose.

....

....

....

....

....

❧ 95 God created the universe as a school—a learning and growing experience for us. You can say love was the creative force.

....
....
....
....
....
....

❧ 96 God is Love, and whenever you reach out in loving kindness, you are expressing God.

....
....
....
....
....

❧ 97 God is Truth and whenever you seek truth, you are seeking God.

....
....
....
....
....

❧ 98 God is Beauty, and whenever you touch the beauty of a flower or a sunset, you are touching God.

....
....
....
....
....
....

❧ 99 God is the intelligence that creates all and sustains all and binds all together and gives life to all.

....
....
....
....
....

❧ 100 God is the essence of all, so you are within God and God is within you—you could not be where God is not.

....
....
....
....
....

❧101 To know God is to feel peace within—a calmness, a serenity, an unshakeableness which enables you to face any situation.

....

....

....

....

....

❧102 To know God is to be so filled with joy that it bubbles over and goes forth to bless the world.

....

....

....

....

....

❧103 Permeating all is the law of God—physical law and spiritual law. Disobey it and you feel unhappiness—you feel separated from God. Obey it and you feel harmony—you feel close to God.

....

....

....

....

....

❧ 104 Heaven and hell are states of being. Heaven is being in harmony with God's will—hell is being out of harmony with God's will. You can be in either state on either side of life. Eventually, all will seek harmony.

....

....

....

....

❧ 105 Nothing threatens those who do God's will, and God's will is love and faith.

....

....

....

....

....

❧ 106 Those who feel hate and fear are out of harmony with God's will and are likely to have difficulties.

....

....

....

....

....

107 There are two things that remove fear from your life. One is real love toward your fellow human beings. You cannot fear that which you really love. The other is a constant awareness of the presence of God.

....

....

....

....

....

108 God's laws can be known from within, but they can also be learned from without, as they have been spoken of by all great religious teachers.

....

....

....

....

....

109 God's guidance can only be known from within. We must remain open to God's guidance.

....

....

....

....

....

❦ 110 God never guides us to break divine law, and if such a negative guidance comes to us we can be sure it is not from God.

....

....

....

....

....

....

❦ 111 Knowing God is not reserved for the great ones. It is for little folks like you and me. God is always seeking every one of us.

....

....

....

....

....

❦ 112 It's my custom to think about God constantly now, but I began by thinking about God last thing at night and first thing in the morning.

....

....

....

....

....

❦113 Communicating with God is a deep inner knowing that God is within you and around you. God "speaks" through the still small voice within.

....

....

....

....

❦114 Although you can perceive some aspects of God mentally and even emotionally, you cannot know God except through an awakening of your divine nature.

....

....

....

....

❦115 You can find God if you will only seek— by obeying divine laws, by loving people, by relinquishing self-will, attachments, negative thoughts and feelings. When you find God it will be in the stillness. You will find God within.

....

....

....

....

❧116 Your own divine nature is actually a drop from the ocean of divine essence around you, and has access to the ocean.

....
....
....
....
....

❧117 From that drop from the ocean of divine essence came all inspired writing in the first place and somebody wrote it down. You yourself can reach out directly into that source.

....
....
....
....
....

❧118 I always have a feeling of awe and wonder at what God can do—using me as an instrument.

....
....
....
....
....
....

*I*n Arizona I began by visiting the Grand Canyon. I saw it in various moods—in bright sunshine, in the fading light of sunset, under a full moon, at sunrise. I could give you its dimensions but that would not make you understand its grandeur. I could tell you about its colors and its unique rock formations—but that would not make you know its beauty. The Grand Canyon cannot be described or even pictured—it must be experienced. I walked to Flagstaff, which is nestled among piñon pines at the foot of Arizona's highest mountain. Then I turned south and walked down, down, down into beautiful Oak Creek Canyon, where the stream flowed swift and clear among the rocks. Then up, up, up I walked over Mingus Mountain and into scenic Prescott.

∞ Four...

On Prayer

❦ 119 We spend a great deal of time telling God what we think should be done, and not enough time waiting in the stillness for God to tell us what to do.

....
....
....
....

❦ 120 I used to walk receptive and silent amid the beauties of nature and these wonderful insights would come to me as I prayed the prayer of receptive silence, which is sometimes called meditation.

....
....
....
....
....

❧ 121 When walking in nature, from the beauty around me I got my inspiration, from the silent receptiveness my meditation, and from the walking both my exercise and my breathing.

....

....

....

....

....

❧ 122 Nature speaks a very strong language— luring us all toward God.

....

....

....

....

....

....

❧ 123 Receptive prayer results in an inner receiving which motivates to right action.

....

....

....

....

....

....

❧ *124* Praying without ceasing is not ritualized, nor are there even words. It is a constant state of awareness of oneness with God along with a constant projection of positive thoughts.

....
....
....
....
....

❧ *125* All right prayer has good effect, but if you give your whole life to the prayer you multiply its power.

....
....
....
....
....

❧ *126* The most important part of prayer is what we *feel*, not what we say.

....
....
....
....
....

❧127 No one really knows the full power of prayer.

....
....
....
....
....
....

❧128 I have discovered that for some who were in very great trouble, the prayer of visualization was helpful to them. You can visualize God's light each day and send it to someone who needs help.

....
....
....
....
....

❧129 One must be very careful when praying for others to pray for the removal of the *cause* and not the removal of the symptom.

....
....
....
....
....

❧ *130* If you have a problem, take the matter to God in prayer, and visualize it in God's hands. Then leave it, knowing it is in the best possible hands.

....

....

....

....

❧ *131* I am constantly thankful. I have this constant feeling of thankfulness, which is a prayer.

....

....

....

....

....

....

❧ *132* I believe nothing is too big to pray for. All good prayer has good effect whether you see the results or not.

....

....

....

....

....

*E*ven though Texas—often referred to as the Lone Star State—is no longer the biggest state, it is still very big. One thing you will surely find in Texas, and that is variety. Western Texas reflects the culture of the West, eastern Texas reflects the culture of the "Deep South," central Texas has a mixed culture. Texas is big enough to include many contrasts. There is much desert in Texas with its cactus and sagebrush, but there is also much water. There are many mountains in Texas, but there is also much low land and much high flat land—and the wide open spaces they talk about are really there in abundance. One thing I found almost everywhere in Texas was friendliness. Friendliness is more than traditional in Texas, it is actual.

∞ *Five...*

On Religion

❧133 Religion is not an end in itself. One's union with God is the ultimate goal.

....

....

....

....

....

....

❧134 Differences between faiths lie in creeds and rituals rather than religious principles.

....

....

....

....

....

....

....

❧ 135 We should try to understand cultural and religious differences—and realize that always our likenesses are greater than our differences.

....

....

....

....

....

❧ 136 When we attempt to isolate another we only isolate ourselves. We are all God's children and there are no favorites.

....

....

....

....

....

....

❧ 137 God is revealed to all who seek; God speaks to all who will listen.

....

....

....

....

....

....

❦ 138 A truly religious person has religious attitudes: a loving attitude toward fellow human beings, an obedient attitude toward God—toward God's laws and God's guidance, and a religious attitude toward self—knowing that you are more than the self-centered nature, more than the body, and life is more than the earth life.

....

....

....

....

....

....

....

❦ 139 One can become so attached to the outward symbols and structure of religion that one forgets its original intent—to bring one closer to God.

....

....

....

....

....

....

....

❧ 140 We have quoted, "Be not overcome of evil, overcome evil with good" and then attempted to overcome evil with more evil, thereby multiplying the evil.

....
....
....
....
....
....
....
....

❧ 141 We worship God, but have no faith in the working of God's law of love. The world awaits the living of the law of love, which will reach the divine within all human beings and transform them.

....
....
....
....
....
....
....
....

❦142 You will note that Jesus says, "Why do you call me 'Lord, Lord' and do not what I say?" Therefore, it seems to me that a real Christian would be living by the laws of God that Jesus taught.

....

....

....

....

❦143 Many people profess Christianity. Very few live it—almost none.

....

....

....

....

....

❦144 On the one hand (people) talk about Christian values, on the other hand they say, "Isn't force the only deterrent they respect?" This has been our trouble down through the ages—we have given only lip service to Christian values.

....

....

....

....

❧ 145 The teaching of divine truth—primarily the law of love—is the religion of the future. It matters not what it is called.

....

....

....

....

....

New Mexico has a sunbaked bleached look. There is much color—yellows and even reds—but it is bleached color. New Mexico has a high look. There are many massive towering mountains, and the unique capital, Santa Fe, is 7,000 feet high. New Mexico has a picturesque look. There are many artistic adobe buildings, and there is a great deal of Indian art. New Mexico has an old look. There is much old Spanish influence. When I reached Albuquerque spring flowers were blooming in the gardens, and I reached Farmington before the frost and saw the apple orchards in full blossom. In the field of peace among groups, New Mexico sets a good example, for many groups live together there quite harmoniously and apparently all groups have equal opportunities.

∞ One...

On Healing

❧ 146 There are two types of healing, whether it is physical healing or otherwise. One is removal of cause, which is good. The other is removal of symptom, which merely postpones the reckoning.

....

....

....

....

....

❧ 147 I pray for the removal of cause instead of the removal of symptom. If only the symptom is removed it will remanifest or another symptom will manifest. This is only postponing the problem.

....

....

....

....

❦148 When you start using Healing Prayer, remember to pray for the removal of cause, not symptom. A simple prayer is, "May this life come into harmony with God's Will."

....
....
....
....

❦149 It is very important to concentrate only on the removal of cause, even though such healings are not as spectacular as the removal of symptoms.

....
....
....
....

❦150 It has been written, "Your faith has made you whole." Enough faith can remove mountains—or symptoms. But my prayer for you is that *cause* will be removed so that your healing will be permanent.

....
....
....
....

❧ 151 Spiritual science believes in spiritual healing which is the removal of cause, rather than psychic healing which is removal of symptoms and only a temporary thing. With God's help you can solve the problem and any other problem that life sets before you.

....
....
....
....

❧ 152 If you are able to put your life completely into God's hands, with a genuine acceptance of God's will, whatever it may be—physical healing may come, and spiritual healing will certainly come.

....
....
....
....

❧ 153 Healing does not always mean staying on this side of life. Sometimes God has other plans for His children—and both sides of life are really one.

....
....
....
....

❦ 154 I never work with sympathy on the removal of the headache or the removal of the pain in the joint or whatever a symptom might be. I use only the prayer that this life will come into harmony with God's will.

❦ 155 I never hesitate to put a person into a healing circumstance—that is, into an uplifting, inspiring circumstance. That can hurt no one.

❦ 156 I do not hesitate to work on the removal of certain things that I know are causes of difficulties. For instance, I don't hesitate to work on the removal of the worry habit or the anger habit or the fear habit.

❧157 I would suggest to people who are in need of healing: beautiful, uplifting music if they relate to beautiful music; the reading of beautiful words if they relate to beautiful words; and I would suggest the beauty of flowers, the beauty of God's nature.

When I first saw Colorado I wrote: It is a sea of towering mountains—many of them snow-capped—and the landscape is so beautiful it is sometimes hard to believe it is real. In Wyoming the mountain peaks did not seem to tower so because I was right up among them, and up there in the grasslands I saw the deer and the antelope play. The remembrance of the grandeur of the western scenery is only surpassed by the remembrance of the many wonderful western friends. In the Dakotas I got the impression of a vast treeless prairie, except for the lovely Black Hills region of South Dakota and North Dakota's Red River Valley. In Nebraska I walked almost every day and spoke almost every evening—and the roads I walked were pleasant roads, with grass on the shoulders and often trees also.

Preparations

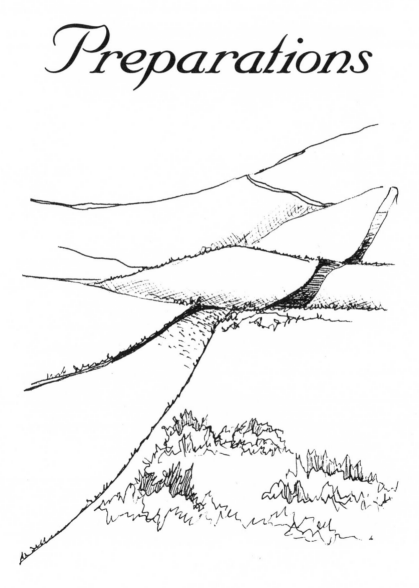

⌒⌒ Seven...

Right Attitude Toward Life

❧ 158 Be willing to face life squarely and get down beneath the surface of life where the verities and realities are to be found.

....
....
....
....
....

❧ 159 Life is a series of tests; but if you pass your tests, you look back upon them as good experiences.

....
....
....
....
....
....

🌿 *160* Concealed in every new situation we face is a spiritual lesson to be learned and a spiritual blessing for us if we learn that lesson.

....

....

....

....

....

🌿 *161* Each season of life is wonderful if you have learned the lessons of the season before. It is only when you go on with lessons unlearned that you wish for a return.

....

....

....

....

....

🌿 *162* When you perceive that problems serve a purpose in your life, you will recognize that problems are opportunities in disguise.

....

....

....

....

....

❦ 163 Every problem that comes to us has a purpose in our life. Through problem solving we learn and grow.

....
....
....
....
....

❦ 164 If only you could see the whole picture, if you knew the whole story, you would realize that no problem ever comes to you that does not have a purpose in your life, that cannot contribute to your inner growth.

....
....
....
....

❦ 165 Recognize all problems, no matter how difficult, as opportunities for spiritual growth, and make the most out of these opportunities.

....
....
....
....
....

❧ *166* If you did not face problems you would just drift through life. It is through solving problems in accordance with the highest light we have that inner growth is attained.

....

....

....

....

....

❧ *167* A life without problems would be a barren existence, without the opportunity for spiritual growth.

....

....

....

....

....

❧ *168* Problems come when we live our lives out of harmony with higher laws—they come to push us toward harmony.

....

....

....

....

....

❧ 169 When societies are out of harmony, problems develop within the society—collective problems. Their purpose is to push the whole society toward harmony.

....
....
....
....

❧ 170 Collective problems must be solved by all of us, collectively, and no one finds inner peace who avoids doing his or her share in the solving of collective problems.

....
....
....
....

❧ 171 Many common problems are caused by wrong attitudes. People see themselves as the center of the universe and judge everything as it relates to them. Naturally, you won't be happy that way.

....
....
....
....
....

❦172 You can only be happy when you see things in proper perspective: all human beings are of equal importance in God's sight, and have a job to do in the divine plan.

....

....

....

....

❦173 It is an orderly universe, and the suffering that comes to us has a purpose in our lives—it is trying to teach us something. We should look for its lesson.

....

....

....

....

....

❦174 Every experience is what you make it and it serves a purpose. It might inspire you, it might educate you, or it might come to give you a chance to be of service in some way.

....

....

....

....

❧175 No problem is set before us that, with a proper attitude, we cannot solve. If a great problem is set before us, this indicates that we have the great inner strength to solve a great problem.

❧176 You must learn to forgive yourself as easily as you forgive others. And then take a further step and use all that energy that you used in condemning yourself for improving yourself.

❧177 Life is like a mirror. Smile at it and it smiles back at you.

ansas, where I had good opportunities to speak at colleges, is a state which I have walked through on every pilgrimage route, so it wasn't surprising that I encountered many old friends there. I think of Oklahoma as an oil state, and I could usually see an oil well or hear an oil pump, and when darkness came there were bright lights in lonely places where well-drilling crews worked all night. In Oklahoma I found I could walk at below zero temperatures. Although there was plenty of snow all around, the highways were fairly clear. In Oklahoma I found much friendliness and much peace interest. One bitter cold morning a college student gave me the gloves from his hands and threw his scarf around my neck. That night, when the temperatures dropped below zero, an American Indian couple gave me shelter.

⚭ *Eight...*

Bringing Your Life into Harmony

🌱178 Divine law can be summed up as the law of love which governs this universe.

....
....
....
....
....

🌱179 The laws which govern this universe work for good as soon as we obey them, and anything contrary to these laws doesn't last long. That which is out of harmony with universal law contains within itself the seeds of its own destruction.

....
....
....
....
....

❦ 180 In a mature society, society's laws would be in harmony with divine law, but we live in an immature world in which society's law is often in flagrant disobedience to divine law.

....

....

....

....

❦ 181 It is up to us to keep our lives steadfastly in harmony with divine law, which is the same for all of us. Only insofar as we remain in harmony with divine law do good things come to us.

....

....

....

....

❦ 182 The good in every human life always makes it possible for us to obey universal laws. We do have free will about all this, and therefore how soon we obey and thereby find harmony, both within ourselves and within our world, is up to us.

....

....

....

....

❧ *183* If your life is in harmony with your part in the Life Pattern, and if you are obedient to the laws which govern this universe, then life is full and life is good but life is nevermore overcrowded. If it is overcrowded, then you are doing more than is right for you to do—more than is your job to do in the total scheme of things.

❧ *184* *This is the way of peace—overcome evil with good, and falsehood with truth, and hatred with love. The Golden Rule would do equally well. These are laws governing human conduct, which apply as rigidly as the law of gravity.*

185 When we disregard the unchanging laws of human conduct, chaos results. Through obedience to these laws this world of ours will enter a period of peace and richness of life beyond our fondest dreams.

....
....
....
....

186 Trust the Law of Love. Since the universe operates in accordance with the Law of Love, how could you trust anything else?

....
....
....
....

187 The lesson of the way of love is that evil can only be overcome by good. We don't need to reach out and tear down the things that are evil because nothing which is contrary to the law of love can endure.

....
....
....
....

❧188 Evil can be helped to fade away more quickly if we remain in obedience to the Law of Love—evil must be overcome with good.

....

....

....

....

....

❧189 Never forget the transforming power of an act done in love—the vibration radiates on and on forever.

....

....

....

....

....

❧190 The power of a kindly word, of a hand clasped in the warmth of spiritual friendship, a simple smile—these things lift the load of a weary and troubled heart.

....

....

....

....

....

❦191 You can rejoice in the times you are called to be an instrument through which God has been able to express infinite love.

....
....
....
....
....

❦192 Every good thing you do, every good thing you say, every good thought you think, vibrates on and never ceases. The evil remains only until it is overcome by the good, but the good remains forever.

....
....
....
....

❦193 Just concentrate on thinking and living and acting in harmony with God's laws and inspiring others to do likewise.

....
....
....
....
....

❦ *194*   Never think of any right effort as being fruitless. All right effort bears fruit, whether we see the results or not.

....
....
....
....

❦ *195*   Be a sweet melody in the great orchestration, instead of a discordant note. The medicine this sick world needs is love. Hatred must be replaced by love, and fear by faith that love will prevail.

....
....
....
....

❦ *196*   People replace the spirit of the law with the letter of the law and truth becomes distorted into falsehood. If you desire confirmation of a truth, it is best to seek it from *within* and not upon a printed page.

....
....
....
....

❧ *197* One who takes the mystic approach receives direct perceptions from within. This is the source from which all truth came in the first place.

....
....
....
....
....

❧ *198* *Evil cannot be overcome by more evil. Evil can only be overcome by good.* It is the lesson of the way of love.

....
....
....
....
....

❧ *199* The contest in the world today is between the old way of attempting to overcome evil with evil, which with modern weapons would lead to complete chaos, and the way of overcoming evil with good, which would lead to a glorious and mature life.

....
....
....
....

200 All not-good things in the world are transient, containing within themselves the seeds of their own destruction. We can help them to fade away more quickly only insofar as we remain in obedience to God's law that evil must be overcome with good.

....

....

....

....

201 Let us help the phoenix to rise from the ashes; let us help lay the foundation for a new renaissance; let us help to accelerate the spiritual awakening until it lifts us into the golden age which would come.

....

....

....

....

202 In order to help usher in the golden age we must see the good in people. We must know it is there, no matter how deeply it may be buried.

....

....

....

....

❧203 It is not through judgment that the good in people can be reached, but through love and faith.

....
....
....
....
....

❧204 Love your fellow human beings—turn to them with friendliness and givingness. Make yourself fit to be called a child of God by living the Way of Love.

....
....
....
....
....

❧205 One in harmony with God's Law of Love has more strength than an army, for one need not subdue an adversary; an adversary can be transformed.

....
....
....
....
....

❦ 206 Pure love is a willingness to give, without a thought of receiving anything in return.

....
....
....
....
....
....

❦ 207 Ultimate peace begins within; when we find peace within there will be no more conflict, no more occasion for war.

....
....
....
....
....

❦ 208 There is within the hearts of people deep desire for peace on earth, and they would speak for peace if they were not bound by apathy, by ignorance, by fear.

....
....
....
....
....

❧ **209** It is the job of the peacemakers to inspire people from their apathy, to dispel their ignorance with truth, to allay their fear with faith that God's laws work—and work for good.

....

....

....

....

....

❧ **210** Those who seem to fail pave the way and often contribute more than those who finally succeed.

....

....

....

....

....

❧ **211** If we fear nothing and radiate love, we can expect good things to come. How much this world needs the message and the example of love and faith!

....

....

....

....

❧ 212 You can only expect to change one person—yourself. After you have changed yourself, your example may inspire others to change themselves.

....

....

....

....

....

❧ 213 The sanctuary of peace dwells within. Seek it out and all things will be added to you.

....

....

....

....

....

....

❧ 214 We limit ourselves by thinking that things can't be done. It's the one who doesn't know it can't be done who does it.

....

....

....

....

....

215 We must walk according to the highest light we have, encountering lovingly those who are out of harmony, and trying to inspire them toward a better way.

....

....

....

....

....

216 From a spiritual point of view, the best way to cope with anything that is out of harmony is never to fear it—that gives it power. Bring good influences to bear upon it; make yourself a good example.

....

....

....

....

217 You have much more power when you are working for the right thing than when you are working against the wrong thing.

....

....

....

....

....

❦218 If the right thing is established the wrong thing will fade away of its own accord because all things that are out of harmony contain within themselves the seeds of their own destruction.

....
....
....
....
....

❦219 Eventually all things that are out of harmony will be destroyed. It is really only how soon that is up to us.

....
....
....
....

❦220 Let the center of your being be one of giving. You can't give too much, and you will discover you cannot give without receiving.

....
....
....
....
....

221 It takes quite a while for the living to catch up with the believing, but of course it can. As we live up to the highest light we have, more light is given.

....
....
....
....
....

I walked in Arkansas in jonquil season—and the jonquils were abundant and lovely. I walked in Arkansas in fruit blossom time—when pear trees were thick with white blooms and dainty pink petals appeared on bare peach boughs and delicate wild plum flowers decorated mountainsides. There is a special beauty in the Ozarks. If you have been there you understand—if you have not been there I cannot explain. There is an old-fashioned friendliness in the Ozarks. People invited me in and offered me various home-grown and homemade foods. People born in Arkansas tend to stay in Arkansas, and when you look from a high ledge across a lake-studded valley to the blue haze-shrouded ledges beyond—and feel the spell of the Ozarks—you understand why.

In Missouri I enjoyed visiting so many old friends and meeting so many new friends. The Ozarks extend into Missouri, and I found myself walking up and down winding roads amid the special beauty of the Ozarks.

∞Nine...

Your Place in the Life Pattern

❧222 Besides God's laws, which are the same for all of us, there is also God's guidance and that is unique for every human soul. If you don't know what God's guidance for your life is, you might try seeking in receptive silence.

....

....

....

....

❧223 All human beings have a calling—which is revealed through an awakening of the divine nature.

....

....

....

....

....

❦224 We are all cells in the body of humanity —all of us, all over the world. Each one has a contribution to make, and will know from within what this contribution is.

....

....

....

....

....

❦225 Of course you have work to do in this world. Your first job is to awaken your own divine nature. You can do that by putting yourself into inspirational circumstances and looking within—and waiting in receptive silence for answers from within.

....

....

....

....

❦226 All human beings are of equal importance in God's sight, and have a job to do in the Divine Plan.

....

....

....

....

227 All people are chosen or called—but we have free will as to whether or not we will follow that calling.

....

....

....

....

228 You begin to do your job in life by doing all of the good things you feel motivated toward, even though they are just little good things at first. You give these priority in your life over all the superficial things that customarily clutter human lives.

....

....

....

....

229 The awakening can take place very early in life. For instance, a child who is to be a musician will know in childhood that music is the way to go.

....

....

....

....

❧230 Your job is something you will be happy doing.

....
....
....
....
....

❧231 If what you are doing is not easy and joyous you can ask yourself two questions: What is my motive for what I am doing? What would I be happy doing?

....
....
....
....
....

❧232 How good it is to earn your livelihood by contributing constructively to the society in which you live—everyone should, of course, and in a healthy society everyone would.

....
....
....
....
....

233 What you do in the present creates the future, so use the present to create a wonderful future.

....
....
....
....
....

234 Concentrate on giving so that you may open yourself to receiving. Concentrate on living according to the light you have, so that you may open yourself to more light.

....
....
....
....
....

235 When you look at things emotionally, you will not see them clearly; when you perceive things spiritually, you will understand.

....
....
....
....
....

❧236 When God guides me to do something I am given strength, I am given supply, I am shown the way. I am given the words to speak.

....
....
....
....
....

❧237 Whether the path is easy or hard I walk in the light of God's love and peace and joy, and I turn to God with psalms of thanksgiving and praise.

....
....
....
....
....

❧238 When you live in constant communication with God, you cannot be lonely. When you perceive the working of God's wonderful plan and know that all good effort bears good fruit, you cannot be discouraged.

....
....
....
....

239 Life is a mixture of successes and failures. Be encouraged by the successes and strengthened by the failures.

240 Live in the present. Do the things that need to be done. Do all the good you can each day. The future will unfold.

241 When you know your part in the scheme of things, in the Divine Plan, there is never a feeling of inadequacy. You are always given the resources for any situation, any obstacle. There is no strain; there is always security.

❄️ **242** When you have found inner peace, you are in contact with the source of universal energy and you cannot be tired.

....
....
....
....
....

❄️ **243** When you have constant communion with God, a constant receiving from within, there is never any doubt; you know your way.

....
....
....
....
....

❄️ **244** All who act upon their highest motivations become a power for good. Know that every right thing you do—every good word you say—every positive thought you think—has good effect.

....
....
....
....
....

❧ 245 From all things you read, and from all people you meet, take what is good—what your own 'Inner Teacher' tells you is for you—and leave the rest.

....
....
....
....
....

❧ 246 For guidance and for truth, it is much better to look to the Source through your own 'Inner Teacher' than to look to people or books.

....
....
....
....
....

❧ 247 Books and people can merely inspire you. Unless they awaken something within you, nothing worthwhile has been accomplished.

....
....
....
....
....

❧248 Forget yourself and concentrate on being of service as much as you can in this world, and then, having lost your lower self in a cause greater than yourself, you will find your higher self: your real self.

....
....
....
....
....

❧249 The God centered nature is constantly awaiting to govern your life gloriously.

....
....
....
....
....

❧250 There are those who know and do not do. This is very sad. If you *know* but do not *do*, you are a very unhappy person indeed.

....
....
....
....
....

❧251 Retirement should mean, not a cessation of activity, but a change of activity with a more complete giving of your life to service. It should therefore be the most wonderful time of your life—the time when you are happily and meaningfully busy.

....

....

....

....

....

I think of Louisiana as a southern state, although its large French population gives it a somewhat different flavor. As I journeyed south I heard many people speaking French, and in New Orleans—which I visited at the beginning of the gay and costly Mardi Gras season—I walked along the narrow streets of the picturesque French Quarter where people were admiring the wrought iron decorations and eating Creole pralines. My Louisiana highway was often bordered by big pine trees with their long soft looking needles shining in the sun, sometimes I walked where the forest floor was carpeted with palmettos, and sometimes where massive live oaks or tall straight cypress trees were thickly hung with Spanish moss—but always I noticed abundant spring flowers in spite of the freeze only a month before.

∽ Ten...

Simplifying Life

252 As you concentrate on giving, you discover that just as you cannot receive without giving, so neither can you give without receiving—even the most wonderful things like health and happiness and inner peace.

....

....

....

253 In this materialistic age we have such a false criteria by which to measure success. We measure it in terms of dollars, in terms of material things. But happiness and inner peace do not lie in that direction.

....

....

....

....

❦ **254** Unnecessary possessions are unnecessary burdens. If you have them, you have to take care of them.

....
....
....
....
....

❦ **255** When you have spiritual security, you have no more feeling of need for material security.

....
....
....
....
....

❦ **256** Faith is a belief in things that your senses have not experienced and your mind does not understand, but you have touched them in other ways and have accepted them.

....
....
....
....
....
....

257 It is easy for one to speak of faith; it is another thing to live it.

....
....
....
....
....

258 People have had to make up for their spiritual impoverishment by accumulating material things. When spiritual blessings come, material things seem unimportant.

....
....
....
....
....

*A*long the grass shoulders along the Mississippi roads walking conditions are ideal, and I met some young men who were trying to walk fifty miles in a day. I know it can be done, because I've done it. In Mississippi the people were warm and friendly and I was given hospitality and good opportunities to speak. As I walked toward Dothan, Alabama I could always see some pine woods somewhere. I could usually see some pecan trees. Things seemed calm in Alabama and I was overwhelmed with hospitality and speaking opportunities. In Georgia I noticed the red earth. The Georgia peach trees were bare but I could not go hungry in Georgia because everywhere there were delicious Georgia pecans. South Carolina is a land of cotton fields and textile mills. I visited many old friends and made many new friends.

Purifications

∞Eleven...

Living Habits

259 It would seem that purification of the body might be the first area in which people would be willing to work—but it is often the last because it means getting rid of our bad habits—something we tend to cling to!

....
....
....
....
....

260 People allow themselves to be slaves of their bad habits and society's bad habits—but they have free will, and if they wish to be free they can.

....
....
....
....

261 Purification of the body means regarding the body as the temple of the spirit and treating it that way.

....
....
....
....
....

262 I have a rule of life that I will not ask anyone to do my dirty work for me. I would never kill a creature or a chicken or even a fish, so I no longer eat flesh.

....
....
....
....
....

263 It says we are given dominion over the creatures of the earth, but it doesn't say we have to be their butchers. We could be the keepers of our lesser brothers.

....
....
....
....

264 We can feed a much greater population than we have, but in order to feed them, we would have to become vegetarian. It takes many times as much land to raise the creature and eat the creature as to raise the vegetable or the fruit and eat that.

....

....

....

....

265 I don't preach vegetarianism more because we haven't even learned not to kill each other yet. I realize we're probably far from a step like this.

....

....

....

....

....

266 If we want to use the body well, for good work, we'll need to treat it like a temple of the spirit and only put into it things that actually will nourish it, will give it strength.

....

....

....

....

❧267 Where food is concerned I practice prevention. Everything that is said to be bad for your health I have cut out long ago. Why wait until you get sick?

....
....
....
....

❧268 There are always two ways of learning things. You either are willing to do the right thing of your own free will or else you refrain from doing the right thing, in which case a problem will come to push you in the right direction.

....
....
....
....

❧269 If there was something I knew very well I shouldn't be doing, I simply quit. I had the good sense to make a quick relinquishment which is the easy way. Tapering off is long and hard and rarely gets accomplished.

....
....
....

❦270   Eat sensibly, eating to live rather than living to eat. Have sensible sleeping habits. Get plenty of fresh air, sunshine, exercise, and contact with nature.

....

....

....

....

❦271   There is a (beneficial) substance in the air left there by the sun which diminishes after the sun goes down and which can be absorbed only while you sleep. Get to bed as soon as possible after the sun goes down.

....

....

....

....

....

❦272   In my frame of reference I am not the body. I am just wearing the body. I am that which activates the body—that's the reality.

....

....

....

....

❧273 Sometimes difficulties of the body come to show that the body is just a transient garment—that the reality is the indestructible essence which activates the body.

....
....
....
....
....

❧274 The earth life is a tiny moment in eternity and yet it's so important. The thing to do is to live it to the best of your ability.

....
....
....
....
....

Iowa in May was lovely with redbud and tulips and other spring blossoms. In Minnesota in June I found tulips and lilacs and iris at their loveliest. In Southern Minnesota there were so many trees, and everything looked so green. In Northern Minnesota there were so many lakes. I noticed how liberated people felt after the long cold winter, and how they really enjoyed the pleasant weather and the pleasant out-of-doors. In Wisconsin there were low rolling hills for scenic beauty, and abundant clear lakes for swimming, and big thick trees for shade. How well I remember my walk along Lake Michigan, where the fresh water waves were rolling in, and where instead of shells there were smooth pebbles of many sizes and colors scattered on the beach.

∽ Twelve...

Thoughts

❧**275** If you realized how powerful your thoughts are, you would never think a negative thought. They can be a powerful influence for good when they're on the positive side, and they can and do make you physically ill when they're on the negative side.

....

....

....

....

❧**276** I don't eat junk foods and I don't think junk thoughts! Let me tell you, junk thoughts can destroy you even more quickly than junk food. Junk thoughts are something to be wary of.

....

....

....

....

❦277 If you're harboring the slightest bitterness toward anyone, or any unkind thoughts of any sort whatever, you must get rid of them quickly. They are not hurting anyone but you.

....

....

....

....

....

❦278 It is said that hate injures the hater, not the hated.

....

....

....

....

....

❦279 Those who get ulcers as a result of hating someone prove to themselves (if they have the eyes to see) that the law of cause and effect works.

....

....

....

....

....

☙ 280 It isn't enough just to do right things and say right things—you must also *think* right things before your life can come into harmony.

....
....
....
....

☙ 281 If we could look a bit more deeply into life, we might see that physical difficulties are reflections of spiritual difficulties, and that negative thoughts and feelings are much more harmful than disease germs.

....
....
....
....

☙ 282 If you realized how powerful your thoughts are, you would never think a defeatist or negative thought. Since we create through thought, we need to concentrate very strongly on positive thoughts.

....
....
....
....
....

❧ *283* If you think you can't do something, you can't. But if you think you can, you may be surprised to discover that you can.

....
....
....
....
....

❧ *284* It is important that our thoughts be constantly for the best that could happen in a situation—for the good things we would like to see happen.

....
....
....
....
....

❧ *285* There is a criterion by which you can judge whether the thoughts you are thinking and the things you are doing are right for you. The criterion is: Have they brought you inner peace?

....
....
....
....

286 Remember the power of thought, and think only about the best that could happen. Dwell only upon the good things you want to see happen.

....
....
....
....

287 All that can ever be predicted is the trend of things. You can never say what the outcome will be, because we are constantly able to turn any prediction in another direction if enough of us get together on that.

....
....
....
....
....

288 When we hear a prediction of some disaster we need to throw the entire weight of our positive thought in the opposite direction!

....
....
....
....
....

❦289 You can work on replacing negative thoughts with positive thoughts. If it is a negative thought about a person, dwell upon a good thing about that person.

....

....

....

....

❦290 If you have a negative thought about a world situation, dwell upon the best that could happen in that situation.

....

....

....

....

❦291 Constantly through thought you are creating your inner conditions and helping to create the conditions around you. So keep your thoughts on the positive side, think about the best that could happen, think about the good things you want to happen.

....

....

....

....

*I*n Illinois I experienced the golden beauty of Indian summer, and watched the maple trees put on their bright autumn raiment. My visit to big, big Chicago was, as always, rather overwhelming. In a week it was possible to just scratch the surface of the opportunities for contacting people there.

How good it is to travel south in the fall of the year, experiencing the tranquil beauty of the harvest time—but staying just ahead of the frost, experiencing the brilliant beauty of the autumn leaves—but traveling on before they are swept from the trees. How good it is to travel north with the spring and to enjoy the spring flowers for several months instead of several weeks. I had both wonderful experiences in the middle of the country.

∽ Thirteen...

Desires

❧292   Since you are here to get yourself in harmony with the laws that govern human conduct and with your part in the scheme of things, your desires should be focused in this direction.

....
....
....
....
....

❧293   It's very important to get your desires *centered* so you will desire only to do God's will for you. You can come to the point of oneness of desire, just to know and do your part in the Life Pattern.

....
....
....
....

❧294 There is a well-worn road which is pleasing to the senses and gratifies worldly desires, but leads to nowhere. And there is the less traveled path, which requires purifications and relinquishments, but results in untold spiritual blessings.

....

....

....

....

....

I walked in Pennsylvania in the fall of the year. I began in the Lehigh Valley. I walked from Easton through Bethlehem, with its star on the hill—through Allentown with its hanging gardens on the lamp-posts—through the mining towns, where there are flower gardens in spite of the scarcity of level ground—through friendly Hazleton, "Pennsylvania's Highest City." Then I went east, ending in Philadelphia, "The Quaker City" as it is sometimes called because it was settled by the peaceful Quakers. In several places in Pennsylvania I noticed the Amish people, with their picturesque clothing and customs. How lovely is Pennsylvania in the autumn. The killing frost came very late, and the flowers were still blooming when I left Pennsylvania in November.

⚭ Fourteen...

Motives

❧ **295** Those who act on their highest motivations become a power for good. It is not important that others be noticeably affected. Results should never be sought or desired.

❧ **296** If your motive is pure greed or self-seeking or the wish for self-glorification, don't do that thing. Don't do anything you would do with such a motive.

❧297 The motive, if you are going to find inner peace, must be an outgoing motive: service. Giving, not getting. Your motive must be good if your work is to have good effect. The secret of life is being of service.

....
....
....
....

❧298 I've met a few people who had to change their jobs in order to change their lives, but I've met many more people who merely had to change their motive to service in order to change their lives.

....
....
....
....

❧299 As you live harmoniously and outgoingly you grow spiritually. In this world you are given as you give.

....
....
....
....

I walked in the state of New York in the spring—from Buffalo to Albany to New York City. I started early enough to see Niagara Falls still in its icy winter coat—a wonderful experience. As I walked through the lovely Finger Lakes region there were pussywillows and crocuses. As I walked through the foothills of the Hudson River there were lilacs and tulips. I spent a couple of busy weeks in the New York City area—met some interesting people and made some good friends. The United Nations building is an imposing sight. I ended my first walk there and was shown around by a United Nations observer. We had a nice little peace walk in New York City, and the wide variety of peace groups there are quite active.

Reliquishments

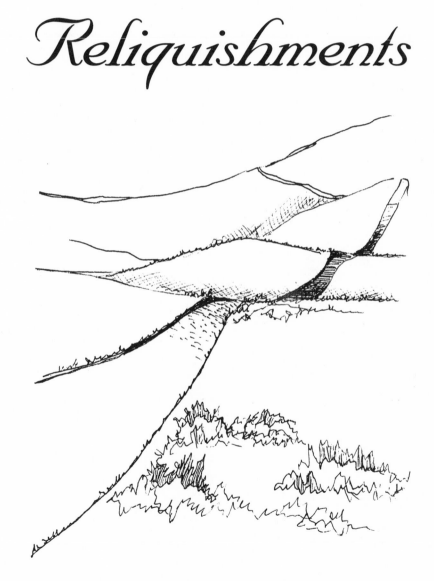

ᴏ⃝ *Fifteen...*

Self-Will

❦300 The self-centered nature is a very formidable enemy and it struggles fiercely to retain its identity. It defends itself in a cunning manner and should not be regarded lightly. It knows the weakest spots of your armor and attempts a confrontation when one is least aware. During these periods of attack, maintain a humble stature and be intimate with none but the guiding whisper of your higher self.

❧ 301 Each of us has free will which we can exercise to become mature—to find inner peace. We must realize that we are completely responsible for our lives. There is no other way.

....
....
....
....

❧ 302 You can work on subordinating the lower self by refraining from doing the not-good things you may be motivated toward—not suppressing them, but transforming them so that the higher self can take over your life.

....
....
....
....

❧ 303 You can deliberately refrain from a bad action—and use the energy for a good action instead.

....
....
....
....
....

304 If you are motivated to do or say a mean thing, you can always think of a good thing. You deliberately turn around and use that *same energy* to do or say a good thing instead. It works!

....

....

....

....

....

305 Bad habits of thought and action lessen as spiritual growth progresses.

....

....

....

....

....

....

306 After you have found inner peace, spiritual growth takes place harmoniously because you—now governed by the higher self—will to do God's will and do not need to be pushed into it.

....

....

....

....

❧307 When you have found inner peace, you have no more feeling of the need to become—you are content to be, which includes following your divine guidance. However, you keep on growing—but harmoniously.

....
....
....
....

❧308 You choose yourself to be a receiver of spiritual truth when you surrender your will to God's will. We all have the same potential.

....
....
....
....
....

❧309 When you surrender your will to God's will you enter a very busy life—and a very beautiful one.

....
....
....
....
....

❦310 God is revealed to all who seek—God speaks to all who will listen.

....
....
....
....
....
....

❦311 When God fills your life, God's gifts overflow to bless all you touch.

....
....
....
....
....
....

❦312 Looking through the eyes of the divine nature you see the essence within the manifestation, the Creator within the Creation, and it is a wonderful, wonderful world.

....
....
....
....
....

I began my 1,000 mile New England pilgrimage in Greenwich, Connecticut and ended in Burlington, Vermont—zigzagging a lot in between to walk through not only the large towns but also the smaller towns to which I had been invited. I started among the apple blossoms—I walked among them when they were pink buds and when their falling petals were white as falling snow. I ended among the ripened apples, which supplied me with some tasty meals. In between I feasted on luscious wild strawberries and blackberries and blueberries. New England is a land of placid lakes and rushing mountain streams and miles and miles of picturesque seacoast with rocks strewn into the sea. New England is a land of hills and mountains, no less scenic than the stately White Mountains of New Hampshire or the rolling Green Mountains of Vermont or the scattered peaks of Maine.

⟡Sixteen...

The Feeling of Separateness

❧313 We begin feeling very separate and judging everything as it relates to us, as though we were the center of the universe. Even after we know better intellectually, we still judge things that way.

....
....
....
....

❧314 We people of the world need to find ways to get to know one another—for then we will recognize that our likenesses are much greater than our differences, however great our differences may seem.

....
....
....
....

❧*315* In reality we are all cells in the body of humanity. We are not separate from our fellow humans.

....
....
....
....
....

❧*316* We can only gain access to the Kingdom of God by realizing it dwells within us as well as in all humanity. Know that we are all cells in the ocean of humanity, each contributing to the others' welfare.

....
....
....
....
....

❧*317* There is a spark of good in everybody, no matter how deeply it may be buried. The real you is that divine spark.

....
....
....
....
....

❧318 It is called by many names: some call it the God-centered nature, others the divine nature or the Kingdom of God within. Psychologists sometimes call it the superconscious. The important thing to remember is that it dwells within you.

....

....

....

....

❧319 Judging others will avail you nothing and injure you spiritually. Only if you can inspire others to judge themselves will anything worthwhile have been accomplished.

....

....

....

....

❧320 It's only from that higher viewpoint that you can know what it is to love your neighbor as yourself. From that higher viewpoint there becomes just one realistic way to work, and that is for the good of the whole.

....

....

....

❧*321* As soon as you begin working for the good of the whole, you find yourself in harmony with all of your fellow human beings.

....
....
....
....
....

f you want to get acquainted with a state try walking 1,000 miles there, which is what I did in Florida. It was a continuous walk, beginning in Pensacola and—after much zigzagging to touch all of the large centers of population—ending in Miami. In the beginning I got acquainted with the Gulf Coast—where the water is such a beautiful green and the sand is so white it looks like snow. In between I got acquainted with a variety of lakes and streams and springs. Most important of all, I got acquainted with lots of friendly people, both natives and visitors. If you want to meet people from all over the United States and Canada, just visit Florida in the winter.

⌒Seventeen...

Relinquishment of Attachments

❧322 Material things must be put into their proper place. They are there for use. It's all right to use them, that's what they're there for. But when they've outlived their usefulness, be ready to relinquish them and perhaps pass them on to someone who does need them.

....
....
....
....

❧323 No one is truly free who is still attached to material things, or to places, or to people.

....
....
....
....
....

❧324 We must be able to appreciate and enjoy the places where we tarry, and yet pass on without anguish when we are called elsewhere.

....

....

....

....

❧325 Anything that you cannot relinquish when it has outlived its usefulness possesses you, and in this materialistic age a great many of us are possessed by our possessions. We are not free.

....

....

....

....

❧326 There is another kind of possessiveness. We do not possess any other human being, no matter how closely related that other may be.

....

....

....

....

327 Only when we realize that we do not possess others, that they must live in accordance with their own inner motivations, are we able to live in harmony with them.

....
....
....
....

328 Anything that you strive to hold captive will hold you captive, and if you desire freedom you must give freedom.

....
....
....
....
....

329 In our spiritual development we are often required to pull up roots many times and to close many chapters in our lives until we are no longer attached to any material thing and can love all people without any attachment to them.

....
....
....
....

❧*330* The path of gradual relinquishment of things hindering spiritual progress is a difficult path, for only when relinquishment is complete do the rewards really come.

....
....
....
....
....

❧*331* The path of quick relinquishment is an easy path, for it brings immediate blessings.

....
....
....
....
....

I first got to Alaska and Hawaii through a wonderful gift from a wonderful friend. Alaska is big and beautiful, wild and wonderful—there is nothing like it anywhere else in the country. I noticed flowers I had never seen in the gardens, and even flowers I was very familiar with looked different. Because of so much daylight, not only flowers, but vegetables, grow to amazingly large sizes. In fact, all that daylight puts so much energy into the air that I felt like running instead of walking. Hawaii was all I thought it would be—and more. I found the July temperature in both Alaska and Hawaii to be between 78 and 82 degrees. Hawaii has what I began to call sun showers, and some of them are really mist showers. Whenever the temperature becomes too high, the mist comes down from the mountains to cool it off. Because of these showers while the sun is shining, Hawaii is a land of rainbows.

∞ Eighteen...

Overcoming Negative Feelings

❦ 332 If you have a loving and positive attitude toward your fellow human beings, you will not fear them.

....
....
....
....

❦ 333 No one walks so safely as one who walks humbly and harmlessly with great love and great faith, for such a person gets through to the good in others (and there is good in everyone), and therefore cannot be harmed.

....
....
....
....
....

❧334 We should never underestimate the great power of the way of love which reaches that spark of good in the other person, always there no matter how deeply buried, and the person is disarmed.

....

....

....

....

❧335 When you approach others in judgment they will be on the defensive. When you are able to approach them in a kindly, loving manner without judgment, they will tend to judge themselves and be transformed.

....

....

....

....

❧336 A loving and kindly approach works between individuals, it works between groups and it would work between nations if nations had the courage to try it.

....

....

....

....

337 Those who choose the negative approach dwell on what is wrong, resorting to judgment and criticism, and sometimes even to name calling. Naturally, the negative approach has a detrimental effect on the person who uses it, while the positive approach has a good effect.

....
....
....
....
....
....
....

338 When an evil is attacked, it mobilizes, although it may have been weak and unorganized before, and therefore the attack gives it validity and strength.

....
....
....
....
....
....
....

❧339 When there is no attack but instead good influences are brought to bear upon a situation, not only does the evil tend to fade away, but the evil doer tends to be transformed.

....

....

....

....

❧340 A positive approach inspires; a negative approach makes angry. When you make people angry, they act in accordance with their baser instincts, often violently and irrationally. When you inspire people, they act in accordance with their higher instincts, sensibly and rationally.

....

....

....

....

❧341 Anger is transient, whereas inspiration sometimes has a lifelong effect.

....

....

....

....

....

❦342 Tremendous energy comes with anger. Do not suppress it: that would hurt you inside. Do not express it: this would not only hurt you inside, it would cause ripples in your surroundings. Transform it: Use that tremendous energy constructively on a task that needs to be done, or in a beneficial form of exercise.

❦343 Some people don't realize that we are required to do everything we can in a situation, and when we come to the point where we can do nothing more, we leave the rest in God's hands.

❧*344* Worry is a useless mulling over of things you can't change—it's a total waste of time and energy.

....
....
....
....
....

❧*345* Worry is not concern—concern is good. Concern leads you to do everything possible in a situation.

....
....
....
....
....

❧*346* If you are worrying, you are either agonizing over the past which you should have forgotten long ago, or being apprehensive over the future which hasn't even come yet.

....
....
....
....
....

❦347 The fear habit is very detrimental because you attract the things you fear. If we have any fear we need to get rid of it.

....

....

....

....

....

❦348 Almost all fear is fear of the unknown. The remedy: *Become acquainted with the thing you fear.*

....

....

....

....

....

❦349 When you find peace within yourself, you become the kind of person who can live at peace with others.

....

....

....

....

....

....

❧350 No outward thing—nothing, nobody from without—can hurt us inside, psychologically.

....

....

....

....

....

❧351 We can only be hurt psychologically by our own wrong actions, which we have control over; by our own wrong reactions—they're tricky but we have control over them, too; or by our own inaction in some situation that needs action from us.

....

....

....

....

....

❧352 We are responsible for our actions, reactions or inaction where action is required. We owe right living not only to humanity, but to ourselves.

....

....

....

....

....

❦353 You have complete control over whether or not you will be hurt psychologically, and any time you want to you can stop hurting yourself.

....

....

....

....

....

❦354 Although others may feel sorry for you, never feel sorry for yourself—it has a deadly effect on spiritual well-being.

....

....

....

....

....

❦355 We tend to skim right over the present moment which is the only moment God gives any of us to live. If you don't live the present moment, you never get around to living at all.

....

....

....

....

....

❦356 Never agonize over the past or worry over the future. Live this day and live it well.

....

....

....

....

....

*T*hroughout the country I saw much superhighway construction, and I noticed that these super-roads tended to run in the valleys, tunneling through the mountains and under the rivers. I'm glad that on my pilgrimage I followed the old roads that climbed the mountains. What wonderful vistas there were to reward those who attained the summit—sometimes views of distant peaks and wooded slopes, sometimes views of buildings or roads where I had walked or would walk, sometimes views of valleys covered with fields and orchards. I know this is an age of efficiency and that superhighways are much more efficient—but I hope there will always be some scenic roads, too—some roads that climb the mountains.

∾Nineteen...

Peace's Beatitudes

❧357 *Blessed* are they who give without expecting even thanks in return, for they shall be abundantly rewarded.

....
....
....
....
....

❧358 *Blessed* are they who translate every good thing they know into action, for ever higher truths shall be revealed unto them.

....
....
....
....
....

❧359 *Blessed* are they who do God's will without asking to see results, for great shall be their recompense.

....
....
....
....
....

❧360 *Blessed* are they who love and trust their fellow beings, for they shall reach the good in people and receive a loving response.

....
....
....
....
....

❧361 *Blessed* are they who have seen reality, for they know that not the garment of clay, but that which activates the garment of clay, is real and indestructible.

....
....
....
....
....

362 *Blessed* are they who see the change we call death as a liberation from the limitations of this earth life, for they shall rejoice with their loved ones who make the glorious transition.

....

....

....

....

363 *Blessed* are they who after dedicating their lives and thereby receiving a blessing, have the courage and faith to surmount the difficulties of the path ahead, for they shall receive a second blessing.

....

....

....

....

....

364 *Blessed* are they who advance toward the spiritual path without the selfish motive of seeking inner peace, for they shall find it.

....

....

....

....

....

❦ 365 *Blessed* are they who instead of trying to batter down the gates of the Kingdom of Heaven approach them humbly and lovingly and purified, for they shall pass right through.

···
···
···
···
···

RENA

Interesting Points in Peace Pilgrim's Life

Throughout her pilgrimage, Peace did not reveal the details of her earlier life, including her name and where she was from. She did this in order to put the emphasis on her message and to protect her relatives from attention. When asked how old she was, Peace would respond, "I have long since put my age out of my mind. I think of myself as ageless, and in radiant health."

Although her message speaks eloquently for itself, the following bits of information may prove useful in understanding her life and personality.

"I had a lot of love in my early life," Peace Pilgrim said. She grew up in Egg Harbor City, New Jersey where she was born in the first decade of the 1900s. She was the oldest of three children, living in an extended family of her parents, siblings and three maiden aunts.

At age three she would hear long poems and often recite them after one hearing. "It was only years later that I realized what the words meant that I was reciting, but I did have this amazing memory."

She learned to read when she was four and therefore said, "When I went to school it was very easy for me to learn to read because I had already done some of it." She loved learning and proved good at it, but considered herself more of a "doer" than a great reader.

She planted her first garden at the age of five when she was given seeds by her parents and grew a beautiful garden of nasturtiums. The next year she was given more kinds of seeds and grew radishes and peanuts.

When she was six a note was sent home to her parents saying she needed to have her tonsils out. Her parents took her in and asked, "What's the matter with her tonsils?" They were told there was nothing wrong but it would be harder on her when she was older. She said, "If there is nothing the matter with them I won't have them out. They must have some purpose." She made such a fuss that her parents acquiesced and she never had them out.

She loved to play the piano. In the summer when she was eight or nine years old she picked up a learning book her grandmother used to teach piano and went right through it. She had learned the top notes in school and taught herself to pick out the bottom notes.

Though she grew up with no formal religious training, her parents taught her to be strictly honest as well as the importance of getting along with people. She first read about the Golden Rule in a history book while still in grade school and it got an inner confirmation from her. "It was different than anything I had ever read before and, therefore, it affected my entire life."

She was first offered cigarettes in grade school and by the upper grades all of her friends drank alcohol and smoked cigarettes. "There was such a push toward conformity in those days that they looked down on me because I didn't." With her peers gathered around her in someone's living room she said, "Look, nobody can stop you from making your choices—but I have a right to make my choices too, and I have chosen freedom." She later went on choose freedom from other enslaving habits also, "..like negative thinking and unnecessary possessions and meaningless activities."

A very daring young person, she loved to swim and dive and would do things like jump off of a bridge into the river below, though she couldn't persuade her companions to join her.

In high school she was on the debating team and a classmate said of her, "She put all she had into it. Even then she was an impressive speaker." She loved drama and wrote and directed plays for a local amateur theatrical group. She continued to be a good student and graduated at the top of her class.

She married in 1933 at the age of 23. Her husband did not share her interests in pacifism and a life of service. Their paths diverged when he went into the armed forces during World War II. The marriage ended in an amicable divorce. Later she would say, "I was not called into the family pattern."

In 1938 she walked all one night through the woods seeking for a meaningful way of life. She walked into a clearing with moonlight streaming down and was moved to offer her life in service. "If you can use me, God, please use me," she prayed.

After offering her life in service she entered into a fifteen-year preparation period which she would later call her "spiritual growing up." During this period of preparation she worked with senior citizens and with people who had problems. She also worked as a volunteer for various peace organizations and published a small newsletter on simple living. For a time she worked on a journal written by Scott Nearing, a champion of simple living.

The year before her pilgrimage began, she walked the entire length of the Appalachian Trail, a two-thousand and fifty mile stretch of rugged, wilderness footpath from Maine to Georgia, carrying only a plastic sheet for the weather and some powdered milk and oatmeal. She was the first woman to walk the full length of the trail. She said of this remarkable feat that it "tends to make you realize what the actual essentials of physical well-being are—such as warmth when you are cold, a dry spot on a rainy day, the simplest food when you are hungry."

Before she started her pilgrimage in 1953 she had attained what she called a permanent state of inner peace. "Finally came the time when I did succeed in leaving the self-centered life. I had slipped out of harmony and when I went to bed that night I thought if I could just remain in harmony I could be of greater usefulness. When I woke up in the morning I was back again on the mountaintop and knew I would never need to descend again into the valley."

With this experience of inner peace she went out for a walk and "a thought just struck my mind. I felt this strong inner motivation toward this next way of witnessing for peace, this pilgrimage." In her mind's eye she saw a vision of her first pilgrimage route, marked in red across a map of the United States.

Peace undertook her pilgrimage in the tradition of pilgrims before her, not to a place, but for a purpose—peace. She didn't carry money nor accept it when it was offered. She walked on faith and found that all of her basic necessities were met. She felt she was "plugged into universal supply," and never went more than three days without food or a place to sleep. She never asked for these things, they were just offered. "Aren't people good!" she would exclaim.

Her pilgrimage was dedicated to "the whole peace picture: peace between individuals, peace between groups, peace between nations, peace with the environment, and of course the very, very important inner peace."

In the beginning she undertook her pilgrimage as a form of penance, which she described as "a willingness to undergo hardships for the achievement of a good purpose" and to concentrate on her prayer for peace. The order of her priorities were walking first, then speaking, and then answering mail. She was a dynamic speaker and spoke to high school and college classes, civic and study groups, service clubs, and in churches of many denominations.

Beginning at Pasadena, California on January 1, 1953, Peace walked west to east across the United States, discarding her original name and details of her earlier life so as to "emphasize the message, and not the messenger." In the years that followed she would take different routes, including one that visited each of the state capitals.

In the second year of her pilgrimage she undertook a forty-five day period of prayer and fasting, taking nothing but distilled water at room temperature. Her fast was a prayer for world disarmament. She took it as a sign and ended her fast after reading in a newspaper of a meeting between President Eisenhower and the prime minister of Great Britain to discuss nuclear disarmament. Shortly after this fast she attained "prayer without ceasing"—the ongoing automatic state of inner prayer described in the anonymous classic, *The Way of a Pilgrim*.

By 1964 she had counted twenty-five thousand miles on foot. She stopped counting miles so that she might walk byways that had no mile markers. Her priorities at that time changed to speaking first, then answering mail and then walking. Many of her speaking engagements were scheduled years in advance. She kept a very disciplined schedule so that people would know where she'd be, and so that she could pick up her mail, which was forwarded to general delivery every week.

In 1979 she led her first "inspirational and educational tour" to Alaska with a group of eighteen people piled into three rented cars. It was an adventure in outdoor living and an opportunity for others to experience a little of what her life was like. In 1980 she led a second inspirational and educational tour, this time to Hawaii. Again it was an outdoor living experience that encompassed four of the islands with eighteen people touring in two rented station wagons.

She was on her seventh pilgrimage route when she made "the glorious transition to a freer life" in 1981. Many people from around the country expressed that the last time they spoke with Peace she was especially radiant. To a few friends she had said, "I feel that the form of my pilgrimage is about to change." She was killed in a head-on collision on a country road near Knox, Indiana, while being driven to a speaking engagement. Peace made the transition on July 7, 1981.

Throughout her 28 years on the road, only a handful of people knew that the person who faithfully forwarded her mail from the little post office in Cologne, New Jersey for nearly three decades was her own sister, Helene.

 Notes...

Ocean Tree Books Peacewatch Editions

From the publisher of Peace Pilgrim

Steps Toward Inner Peace: Principles for Harmonious Living
Peace Pilgrim   *Keepsake Edition.* 0-943734-24-X, 64 pages $8.00
Peace Pilgrim: Her Life and Work in Her Own Words
Hardcover Edition.   ISBN 0-943734-20-7, 224 pages $14.95
Peace Pilgrim: Her Life and Work in Her Own Words
Softcover Trade Edition. ISBN 0-943734-29-0, 224 pages $12.00
Gandhi's Seven Steps to Global Change
Guy de Mallac   ISBN 0-943734-16-9, 64 pages $7.95
Gandhi Through a Child's Eyes: An Intimate Memoir
Narayan Desai   ISBN 0-943734-23-1, 64 pages $8.00
The Community of the Ark: Lanza del Vasto's Gandhian Retreat
Mark Shepard   ISBN 0-943734-28-2, 64 pages $8.00
Victories Without Violence: Overcoming Dangerous Situations
Ruth A. Fry   ISBN 0-943734-06-1, 88 pages $6.00
A Road to the Future: Complete Text of the United Nations Address
Mikhail Gorbachev   ISBN 0-943734-13-4, 48 pages $5.95
The Great Peace March: An American Odyssey
Franklin Folsom   ISBN 0-943734-14-2, 208 pages $10.95
Peace Like a River: A Personal Journey
Sue Guist   ISBN 0-943734-17-7, 224 pages $8.95

OCEAN TREE BOOKS

Post Office Box 1295, Santa Fe, New Mexico 87504
(505) 983-1412

Spiritual Titles from Blue Dove Press

Messages of the sages and saints of all traditions

Treasury of Spiritual Wisdom
Compiled by Andy Zubko   ISBN 1-884997-10-4, 528 pages, $19.95

Hearts on Fire: The Tao of Meditation
Stephen Wolinski   ISBN 1-884997-25-2, 194 pages, $14.00

In Quest of God: The Saga of an Extraordinary Pilgrimage
Swami Ramdas   ISBN 1-884997-01-5, 190 pages, $10.95

In the Vision of God, Vol. I: The Continuing Saga
Swami Ramdas   ISBN 1-884997-03-1, 288 pages, $14.95

In the Vision of God, Vol. II: The Conclusion
Swami Ramdas   ISBN 1-884997-05-8, 280 pages, $14.95

The Play of God: Visions of the Life of Krishna
Vanamali   ISBN 1-884997-07-4, 416 pages, $19.95

The Ultimate Medicine As Prescribed by Sri Nisargadatta Marjaraj
Robert Powell, editor   ISBN 1-884997-09-0, 240 pages, $11.95

The Nectar of Immortality: Sri Nisargadatta Majaraj on the Eternal
Robert Powell, editor   ISBN 1-884997-13-9, 200 pages, $14.00

The Experience of Nothingness
Sri Nisargadatta Marjaraj   ISBN 1-884997-14-7, 180 pages, $ TBA

Dialogues on Reality
Robert Powell   ISBN 1-884997-16-3, 190 pages, $14.00

BLUE DOVE PRESS

Post Office Box 261611, San Diego, California 92196
(800) 691-1008